The Essential Derk Wynand

The Essential Derk Wynand

selected by John Barton

The Porcupine's Quill

Library and Archives Canada Cataloguing in Publication

Title: The essential Derk Wynand / selected by John Barton.
Other titles: Poems. Selections
Names: Wynand, Derk, author. | Barton, John, 1957– editor.
Series: Essential poets (Erin, Ont.) ; 21.
Description: Series statement: Essential poets ; 21 | Includes bibliographical references.
Identifiers: Canadiana (print) 20200285130 | Canadiana (ebook) 20200285211 | ISBN 9780889844407 (softcover) | ISBN 9780889848740 (PDF)
Classification: LCC PS8595.Y58 A6 2020 | DDC C811/.54—dc23

1 2 3 • 22 21 20

Published by The Porcupine's Quill, 68 Main Street, PO Box 160, Erin, Ontario NOB 1TO. http://porcupinesquill.ca

'Airborne', 'Table Talk', 'Status of Beggar in Old Havana' and 'An Ideal Place' from *Past Imperfect, Future Tense* are reprinted with the permission of Bayeux Arts, Calgary.

Copyedited by Chandra Wohleber. Represented in Canada by Canadian Manda. Trade orders are available from University of Toronto Press.

We acknowledge the support of the Ontario Arts Council and the Canada Council for the Arts for our publishing program. The financial support of the Government of Canada is also gratefully acknowledged.

Canada Council for the Arts | Conseil des arts du Canada

Canada

ONTARIO ARTS COUNCIL
CONSEIL DES ARTS DE L'ONTARIO
an Ontario government agency
un organisme du gouvernement de l'Ontario

Ontario
Ontario Media Development Corporation

Table of Contents

Foreword

In the fall of 1965, Derk Wynand's decision to enroll in a two-semester-long writing workshop during the final year of his undergraduate degree in English and philosophy more than likely changed the direction of his life. He was twenty-one years old. By the time he graduated from the University of British Columbia the following April, his inclination to write poetry was sufficiently well rooted. In September 1967, the year of Canada's centenary and the crystallization of 'CanLit' into a self-obsessed national preoccupation, he would return to UBC to embark upon postgraduate studies in creative writing. A mandatory course in translation led by Michael Bullock exposed Wynand to contemporary modes of expression less commonly pursued by writers solely anchored in Anglo-American modernism.

Of course, by blood, Wynand is not of English, English-Canadian, or American origin. Born in Germany in 1944, he emigrated with his family to Canada, settling in Vancouver in 1952. As he adapted to his new home and began to learn English, Wynand would find that his identity as a 'German-Canadian', especially in terms of language, truly had become 'hyphenated'. Progressively more habituated to speaking English in place of German, he would find that '[w]ords do not always say what they mean, nor mean what they say; language is not always stable, nor, it seems, is the world.'[1] His unequal fluency in two not wholly alike languages may have promoted this self-described 'existential anxiety', but, by the time he started his MA, it proved to be a carrot. '[F]or me, German heritage really means a receptivity to things German, an "inclination" to explore the works of Brecht, Aichinger, Grass, even if they sometimes happen to be works in English translation.'[2] With Bullock's encouragement as well as that of UBC faculty member J. Michael Yates, he incorporated translation into a lifelong writing practice[3], not only translating German and French writers into English but sometimes also applying their techniques to the composition of his own poetry. His time at UBC equipped him with a poetic toolkit assembled from traditions, European *and* Anglo-American, that he would expand through the course of his literary career.

It is Wynand's wide-ranging use of this toolkit that makes his poetry so compelling. A discussion about the scope of his literary explorations is best entered into via H.C. Artmann. Wynand first encountered the twentieth-century Austrian writer's poetry and prose while browsing the UBC library's stacks to find poetry and prose to translate for Michael Bullock's class. His influence was, by Wynand's admission, 'osmotic'.[4] In issues of *Merkur* and *Akzente*, 'I found some of the ghazal-ish poems of Artmann's, whose playfulness and leaping connections appealed to me.' His translation of 'i am a polar constellation' showcases these qualities: 'i am a polar constellation i cost a hundred dollars / a polar bear bore me on a winter's night twinkling // I buy my furs in the best stores of alaska / i say good frost while shopping....'[5] At around the same time, Wynand wrote 'skating down a dutch canal', a similarly ghazal-like poem that five years later he collected into 1974's *Snowscapes*: '... what do you think of snow / on ice over water or brimstone and fire do you hunger // for edam cheese gouda and bittersweet chocolate or the / red cheeks of that young woman behind you much sweeter....'

Wynand refined Artmann's approach to the couplet in 1983's *Second Person*, which Stephen Scobie describes aptly as 'adopt[ing] the arbitrary technical demand that the two lines of each couplet be, in typewriter spacing, exactly equal in length ... so that the lines look like justified prose.'[6] Like Artmann, Wynand eschews all punctuation and capitalization, adding a further requirement that all line and stanza breaks be determined solely by the line's preestablished letter count — a compendium of constraints that 'Reconstruction' exemplifies: 'after such fires and counts of the dead no one foretells / that the smoke will clear that they will let go of their // claims and what claims them diamonds letting go of their / necks and fingers the titles forgetting the men who have // held them....' The effect is hypnotic; of the reader the poems in *Second Person* ask for total immersive engagement in order to negotiate and grasp the import of Wynand's stripped-down syntax, which slows the eye and races the heart. With the exception of *Love Alone* by American poet Paul Monette[7], which similarly eschews many of poetry's recognizable technical conventions to regulate flow, I can think of no contemporary poetry in English quite like *Second Person*. Wynand's translation of Artmann's 1967 collection, *Fleiss und Industrie*[8], points to another shared quality that Wynand gives explicit voice to in *Snowscapes* and in the 1980 poetic-prose novel, *One Cook, Once Dreaming*: a complete evocation of self-contained worlds built incrementally. Of course, Artmann's influence never proscribed any others; Borges, Calvino, Kafka, and the Brothers Grimm likewise ballast Wynand's sometimes surreal, sometimes folkloric allegories.

After the magical poetic prose of *One Cook, Once Dreaming* and the breathless lines of *Second Person*, Wynand does not rest in his formal experimentation. *Fetishistic*, a collection of acerbic, short-lined, mostly single-page lyrics published in 1984, forswears the employment of active verbs, instead relegating them to more compromised, passive appearances in secondary clauses. The poems' one-word titles, which read as nouns but are also verbs, 'were a way of sneaking the verb into poems that otherwise hide the verbal inside participles or gerunds.' According to Bruce Whiteman, 'It is the idea of words themselves as fetishes, language as an inanimate source of power that alone is capable of releasing for the heart and the mind the presence of a thing or occurrence.'[9] In contrast, 1992's tour de force, *Airborne*, is a single eight-page-long sentence that, as Wynand describes it, launches 'a novice pilot going out on his first solo flight, running out of gas, and then keeping on flying anyway ... [a] ramble without rambling too much.' The poem's shifts, which buffet the narrator from the personal to the political to the mythic, reprise in realist terms the cosmological broad strokes of *Snowscapes* and *One Cook, Once Dreaming*. Those broad strokes are miniaturized, even if only superficially in the poems' lengths, in the books that Wynand released in 1997, 2002, and 2010, *Closer to Home*, *Dead Man's Float*, and *Past Imperfect, Future Tense*. Each gathers deftly written free-verse poems that surround and occasionally erode domestic comfort with an uneasy awareness of a larger world destabilized by war, environmental degradation, and social inequities, the last of which are well represented by 'Status of the Beggar in Old Havana'.

If a single theme unifies Wynand's twelve books and chapbooks, it is love. Every formal device he has employed across five decades of writing variously unpacks Eros, psychologically, erotically, and empathically, while paralleling the through-line of his marriage to his wife, Eva, who some could argue stands as his muse. It is his recognition of the beloved's equal agency, however, that allows his poems to resist any unsympathetic misreading of them as anachronistic by-products of the male gaze. 'A Kind of Spring Fever' is characteristic: husband and wife are delightedly engaged in playful debate. In his 1988 collection, *Heat Waves*, the couple at its core are thrown even more closely together than normal while living away from home in Portugal for an extended period. Their ever-deepening intimacy allows Wynand to most fully articulate the proximities and solitudes of established relationship. While his other books may contain poems that often more emphatically startle, *Heat Waves* is perhaps Wynand's most contentedly visceral book, where, according to Thomas Carpenter in *Books in Canada*, 'regular everyday people, who have neighbours and bugs in their homes, also have periodic magic and poetry in their lives.'[10] The unstable world that Wynand thought language did not wholly mitigate when he spoke at Germanica 88, coincidentally in the same year that *Heat Waves* appeared, is to some extent assuaged by the solaces of intimacy that this exquisite book touches on, an intimacy that more often than not needs no language at all to be deeply felt or shared. As 'Crosswords' concludes: 'Some things refuse / to fit into language. Churches, he says, / should haul down their bells, give it a rest. / A silence, she says, in music, four letters, thank you.'

1. Derk Wynand, 'My German Heritage,' presented at Germanica 88, Vancouver, April 23, 1988, p. 4.
2. Ibid., p. 3.
3. Wynand is a rarity among translators. Most translate into their first language; he translates into his second.
4. Unless otherwise indicated, all quotations are drawn from Wynand's replies to questions I posed to him by email in February and June 2020.
5. H.C. Artmann, 'i am a polar constellation', Derk Wynand, tr. *Contemporary Literature in Translation* 1, 1968, 22–23.
6. Stephen Scobie [Review of *Second Person* and *Fetishistic*], *The Malahat Review*, Fall 1984, 125–26.
7. Paul Monette, *Love Alone: Eighteen Elegies for Rog*. New York: St. Martin's, 1988.
8. H.C. Artmann, *Sweat and Industry*, Derk Wynand, tr. London: Atlas, 1992.
9. Bruce Whiteman, 'Objects of Adoration'. *Writers Quarterly* 7(1), 1985, 23.
10. Thomas Carpenter, 'Heat Waves', *Books in Canada*, January 1989, 6.

Man, Woman, and Boat

The horizon
and water at her foot seem
almost empty.

Emptiness seems sharper here,
a precision between
woman and man.

Naked, the man in the boat
draws toward
the woman in the water.

Urgency of rudder,
not shame,
places his hand.

Fear of water,
not virginal craft,
hoists her dress past the knee.

Surely, the distance closes.
Nothing on the man's face
tells everything about the man.

Her face given to the man,
no one can guess
the woman.

from *Snowscapes*

*

He sleeps on top of the sheet she sleeps under, both covered by a quilt of interlocking hexagons knit of virgin wool and sewn together with a white thread. Each dreams dreams nightly, in colour — they know because even though they dream mostly of snow and of snow figures, the latter cast, in the dream, a distinct blue shadow they distinctly remember. Frequently, his dreams feature snowmen with carrots for noses, which really means, he assumes come morning, the raptures of childhood. She is less precise, in her dreams as in their telling, sensing rather a pink husk, warm and soft, from a time before sheets. Rarely, while dreaming, they touch, separated only by the thin sheets their bodies have, each from its own side, warmed. Then it is as if an orange object he recalls clearly were making contact with a pink tissue she guesses always, touching without merging, like snowflakes that retain their identity for all their falling. On such mornings, they are secretly glad for their parallel, if not entirely equal dreams, glad for the blanket that keeps them equally warm.

from *Snowscapes*

*

skating down a dutch canal what do you think of snow
on ice over water or brimstone and fire do you hunger

for edam cheese gouda and bittersweet chocolate or the
red cheeks of that young woman behind you much sweeter

can you hear a rhythmic breathing the hiss of her skate
and does it remind you of calvin does that disturb you

would it if you were not skating down a dutch canal can
you concentrate on red lips and blondeness or merely on

snow-covered windmills on whitewashed houses now do you
imagine her inside and you the would-be lover her pious

father staying up late reading hebrew never a man to
put up with bundling do you picture him at work cutting

diamonds for african merchants does it trouble you to
think about jewels cut for swiss watches would it be

easier to recall his love for all germans his daughter
skating behind you singing of claus and of marsman their

worship of cheese as you skate in a straight line to
rotterdam sister city of zurich where you loved her

Observation

How the light breaks when it does.

How the eye takes in the light breaking.

How the brain corrects the upside-down image
if that's what it does.

How the mountain's reflection on the lake water
resembles the mountain.

How you become less and less certain.

If you throw a stone, how the water ripples.
How the reflected mountain becomes rippling water only.

How the water becomes smooth again.

How your uncertainty returns if it does so.

How your brain tricks your body
into thinking itself absent.

How water must do just that for stone.

Chagall

Helium. Hydrogen. All
the laughing gases, lighter
than air, more explosive
than buds of white flowers
in a hand. All that white
love waiting for fire,
what he can't show
without floating in air
like flowers exploding,
laughing like gases, head-
over-heels always
toward her. She takes them
like flowers, not fire,
taking the same air,
helium, hydrogen, all
the laughing gases exploding
inside her. White detonations.
White fire inside him.
And they burst like head-
over-heels lovers,
lighter than air.

What I Remember

Of bread soup
I remember only
the shape of
the spoon and
the darkness of
the cellar. Of
the women who
held the ladles
I remember only
the salt in
their voices. Of
my teachers I
remember best of
all: you, reminding
me nightly of
the words for
night, breaking like
dark bread over
which you spread
stars, saying welcome.

from *One Cook, Once Dreaming*

...

'The visiting poet's just kissed me on the ear,' the cook's wife tells her husband.

'Don't let it go to your head,' he tells her, aware of the dangerous thoughts to which a barbed poet's actions can give rise, thoughts she would do better to reserve for her most intimate journal. But then he considers that little harm can be done by a whiskered kiss on the ear, more elusive than a clandestine word uprooted from a poet's world, a trope high on the pyramid of language, in such a rarefied air that not even a worm could survive there, not even the millipede his wife shuns because it rolls itself into a noxious ball when threatened, because its reproductive organs are located in front. Yes, he understands well these fears of his wife's, for she has no lock to protect the intimacy of her journal. Not everything makes him jealous.

'He wants me to sit still for him,' she says, not thinking about pyramids or millipedes. 'He wants to capture my essence in approximate dactyls.'

'Poets have always had ideas,' the cook tells her, remembering his own adolescence. He balls his hand into a fist to remain in control, nibbles on the nape of her neck in such an artful way that she whispers, for his ears alone: 'Let's go home just as quickly as our four legs can take us.'

Reconstruction

for my brother

after such fires and counts of the dead no one foretells
that the smoke will clear that they will let go of their

claims and what claims them diamonds letting go of their
necks and fingers the titles forgetting the men who have

held them while bricks fall in on ancient deeds the hold
on things the hold of things broken like the portals and

doors the towers and city walls and the books and albums
give up their worms the registers renounce their numbers

falling or burning to the ground turning history beneath
the historical guns which lay flat bunker and church and

what they've stood for any number of values counting for
nothing dismembered the broken walls let go the memories

the certainty that life because it is what it is will go
on other than it is and poems long unread will never can

never again be written and mere paint will burn hand and
canvas alike so who will begin to conceive of new cities

who foresee that the mind will relinquish its nightmares
to dream on nor can one say before the smoke has cleared

and the dead lie numbered that if they are not what some
claim them to be they are more than smoke in that smoke-

filled air are left their hunger for the daily bread and
a spasm in the jaw for prayers left their dry impatience

in bread lines or a knowledge of borders shifting faster
than pen over paper left their dreams of defeat when the

stomach grants the brain its thoughts and time for guilt
to be accomplished given a memory of the shadow of wings

within the shadows thrown by remembered fire they try to
say the air at least and the smoke are ours the ocean is

nothing if not charted blue the water white the wind and
osterode's let go hannover let go rotterdam le havre the

white cliffs of dover let go whoever sees none speaks of
the justice in their oil-powered ocean journey the smoke

settling like a disturbing thought across their wake the
horizon pitching around them containing whatever may lie

behind and ahead as some look back and others look ahead
none talking never talking the mind too full for talking

no subject fit to be talked of theirs not yet a language
for talking as only the women in the cabins seasick sick

of everything that refuses to give up its name sick with
the dead morning sick only the women summon the children

who would rather be on deck watching schools of dolphins
to teach them the new the necessary words for there will

be talking again and the men lean over railings elbow to
elbow silence to silence each locked into his individual

sickness taking in the rolling of the wide water and the
gusts of white wind or perhaps they see dolphins as they

bend to the water not talking or talking of dolphins and
some might try to express their dreams pressing unsteady

hands into the air that for the time they merely breathe
as the mouth of the st lawrence defies their predictions

the absence of icebergs *in kanada ist keiner da* and then
predictions are let go by nightfall certain grey tissues

still marked by dying fires or gazing at the unpromising
constellations including delphinus they recall the day's

shores new islands with their distant woods so much wood
to be cut and the tar-papered churches with the aluminum

roofs run down and for all that new much that is new and
they dream they must dream of building of good lumber of

land of log cabins country houses ranches farms dreaming
of construction they reach solid ground as no band plays

welcoming songs then the too solid ground set in its own
ways then washing dishes or inspecting concrete and long

strolls in the free parks then conifers letting go their
endless cones then the impossible prices then impossibly

white bread then kidney and potatoes potatoes and kidney
then saving each penny then more potato than kidney then

clearing sections of land then breaking the solid ground
then more digging then saving each penny then a familiar

ring of hammer or spade then three shovels of gravel for
one of cement then roof walls kidney and potatoes then a

certain pride on walks in the free parks then the window
receiving its glass and the door receiving its bolt then

saving every penny then curtains behind which to dream a
private dream then waking stresses on wood and bone then

fences then walking in free parks then keeping the voice
low in public places then talking the free language then

working at better jobs and not talking again then saving
every second penny then sleeping with easier dreams then

talking in sleep now and then laughing and laughing more
often then the good smoke rising from a good chimney and

the children grow tall like children stealing matches to
stuff into spent shotgun shells creating smoke bombs and

they are not thieves and their parents don't feel robbed
and in the nearby woods they bury potatoes raising small

fires above them then as the potatoes bake and the fires
burn down they talk talking freely with barely an accent

and this is our own reconstruction an image clearer than
most of those others you and me by the good fire talking

Five Tattoos and One Suggested

the new dancer nudge nudge is she part gypsy is she half
japanese confines her routine to the stage how your mind

begins to wander she cannot she will not pick coins from
your table or dollar bills or cigarettes or rough drafts

of poems on serviettes without bringing hands or fingers
into play which does not mean her routine falls short of

your expectations but the imagination keeps tricking you
you don't feel tricked and if she's heard of stunts with

your glasses with johnson's baby oil what's left of your
beer she ignores it likely being wet behind the ears not

having travelled abroad at the end of the war not having
seen what others have seen widows dancing for less maybe

cigarettes or small potatoes not underfed she won't bend
over backward is she japanese certainly not for you when

your wife seems to whisper at your side which is another
fiction entirely the dancer has a kind of decorum is she

japanese she has a boyfriend of sorts tormented by guilt
who's older who cups his hand over his mouth and reveals

his humiliating weakness to the bartender who hands over
the girlfriend's pay not that she is his slave a hundred

dollars your wife says wide-eyed two red fifties she has
a great eye for such details though she could only guess

like you if she were guessing what it would take to make
the dancer vary her strict routine once you'd never have

dragged your wife into a beer parlour like this nor into
your poems she's nobody's slave though her eye can prove

helpful you had a certain decorum because of your german
background maybe because of her own but she has a better

vision she has her own devices and life was simpler once
your poems not running on and on less complex less wordy

have it as you will a dancer out of nowhere slipping off
her blouse it's hot beneath the red stage lights turning

the skin nearly flawless only marked for now by a spider
clinging to her breast stunned by the light maybe calmed

by the involuntary not unwilled agitations not biting or
having bitten already the cadence livelier more frenzied

if better now more tarantella than bump and grind though
the woman does not appear alarmed she is inscrutable she

is a gypsy no doubt she's never studied archaic european
nervous disorders but the audience feels short of breath

a collective heart rate increasing is this spider a mark
of slaves a secret number or name disguised made all too

ornate still making you break into a sweat you have seen
what you've seen girls dancing for less don't lapse into

a coma your wife says not overly impressed by the marked
flesh looking glumly at the few bills that remain on the

table you have bought nothing but beer she's hungry life
was simpler once you could take in a performance without

pinpointing spiders on a half-japanese stripper's breast
to incorporate into your poem as justification expiation

or listening for some voice to say ye shall not make any
cuttings in your flesh let my people go your mouth could

go dry for its own reasons a guilt-ridden paramour would
never have played any part not demanding that she follow

him to the tattoo parlour the designs already cut in his
mind her shorts dropping to the floor into the red light

it is too hot you could roll up your sleeves and a cobra
flares its hood along her spine sways back and forth and

back and forth about to strike striking your wife admits
and that is what it is *tattow tatau tattaw* a knocking or

striking and then she is totally exposed the dancer that
is but for these blue cuttings these marks that make you

so nervous is it your somber mid-european background the
cobra has no tail at all coiling down her spine slipping

deeper into her flesh its hood flaring across her lumbar
region very striking with its counterfeit eyes its fangs

truly venomous attractive and repulsive at the same time
wonderful confusion you imagine the double needle fixing

the outline the multiple needle shading it in is it your
background that makes the breath so laboured her passive

skin tortured at the parlour don't lapse into a coma the
tattooist must have said we can finish it later you make

the connections your heart rate increasing the boyfriend
the spider the cobra electric needle buzzing your german

background all make you nervous how much easier to think
of the japanese art of *irezumi* and the lovely skins that

hang in the museum of tokyo university paid for when the
human exhibits were walking and bathing were resplendent

maybe dancing less naked and you have bought nothing but
rounds of tuborg beer the dancer inscrutable now bending

over backward the boyfriend's been paid nudge nudge more
gypsy now than german your wife points out to you a tiny

red flower growing on her thigh too small to define with
any precision an amaryllis you assume yes the belladonna

dilating your eye it could be the standard rose from the
tattooist's wall its thorn if not poisonous yet adequate

connection careful your wife says the boyfriend's at the
bar eyeing the bartender each has one small blue swallow

marked on his wrist to what secret order can they belong
they are sweating staring at the two of you reading your

thoughts have you found them out have they found you out
why did you bring your wife into the place can she dance

be careful she says the girl's protected by her venomous
creatures drink up the beer at least is already paid for

it's hot you might roll up your sleeves you have nothing
to hide how well she understands you the spider's asleep

on the dancer's breast she's naked as can be the cobra's
fixed on her back the belladonna is gathering its poison

A Kind of Spring Fever

if i came back as a flower would you pick me if i spoke
says eva my wife of course i reply so long as i can use

it in the poem what kind of flower be concrete linnaeus
you know and imagery iris she says hopefully iris i say

how would *that* sound a verbal iris if i returned as one
believe me she says i'd be eloquent your instincts have

always been good i say hardly believing in eloquence in
poetry however and unsure besides of the current status

of the eternal return well would you pick me then among
all those others eva says you have finally at long last

after all the years etc told me about be specific i say
thinking about this poem laurie she says hannah suzanne

you name them so i do testing their assonance naturally
i'd pick you as i've done already and especially if you

spoke but what would you say that i'd pick you also she
says over jürgen and peter and stop i say not caring to

burden the poem with inessential detail specificity has
limits be fair she says not concerned in the least with

my poetics you named *three* very well then jim i say jim
from california are you happy now the poem is fair it's

perfectly balanced from l a she adds wilshire boulevard
to be precise where did you meet suzanne rue dorchester

i answer lying through my teeth what did she say as you
picked her out from all the others did she say *mon cher*

what others i say with a sense of *déjà entendu* now come
on she says there were plenty in montreal it was winter

i say january 67 to be exact in that season the flowers
speak no language that we could ever hope to understand

Word

In the tide pool, the anemone,
closing its mouth around
your pen or finger poking.

The obvious symbols.

The woman, saying, *The anemone*
opens and closes its mouth,
never saying a word.

The message conveyed
for all that.

The wind rose in her hair.
Her preference for the anemone
open. The inevitable connections.

The woman making them, saying,
Look how it anticipates
the tip of your pen.

As if it were conscious.

These words, words falling
between you.

Silhouette

Ice branches, turning
to mist on the pane.

The clear water clouding
in the inviolate glass.

These relentless miracles
marked well: the cuttings
taken by day, the troublesome
water changed daily.

The woman at night, sleeping away
from you, an arm's length only,
an adequate distance,

keeping one eye open
to the window, in which April
light sharpens to June.

You, waiting for a thief, cut
asters bunched in his hand,
a silhouette only, but of

a reliable thief, eyeing
the silver, polished, the china set
out for him, the woman blushing
toward him,

breathing new life into the cut
shadows, unaware of your mouth,
urging the black of his fingers
to steal nothing, nothing
but her dream away.

Cinch

Cinch
that it is

to which you give up
your breathing, freely,
notch by notch,
freely

saying to the woman,
wheezing, *Tighter!*

The soft body
stocking perfectly
adjusted,

as in Vienna the doctors
are saying, *Junge, Junge,*
slapping their knees.
So eine Freude!

Tighter. Your belly, chest,
head constrained,
concentrated on themselves,
not Vienna with its
élitist cafés,

from which the women
gladly excuse themselves.

Figure

These numbers shifted by a pencil
over paper, the sums neither increased
nor reduced to your liking.

What they account for not urgent.

The columns juggled. The new combinations
tried. The equation not changing:

such the miracle of this calculus.

Your office window shut to the marked,
substantial things, to hold their stench
away, a curtain drawn across to block
the animate light and shadow,

the stinking source of your calculations.
The bodies diseased, not dying
efficiently enough.

Your pencil jabbed into the paper:
a needle killing all pain.

The bullets in the chamber: one for
yourself, one for your wife, one for each
of your straw-haired children.

The urgency of this simpler reckoning,
as the numbers smudge into nothing
but carbon. The columns not stinking
to high heaven. Your window shut

to the forces outside, keeping that world
and the inner world in such
excellent balance.

Earthquake

Last night, the earth took our house
and gave it a good shaking: the European
skylarks started up from the TV antenna;
the vertical hold did not hold; the mice
stopped rolling walnuts down the aluminum
ducts in the basement. Doors rattled
in their frames as though someone
desperate wanted in or out and we
refused to open; the windows threatened
to shatter. The rocking chair rocked
before the fireplace, no fire in it,
but only the soot drifting down. The pipes
played a new tune behind the walls.
As our bed shook, we clung to each other
because, for the first time in our life,
our lives seemed to depend on it. The bed
shook; the chair at its foot shook; the lamp,
tungsten buzzing, swung back and forth
on its chain. We held on tight, labouring
to breathe, neither of us able to come up
with a word that could correctly name
the situation in which we suddenly found
ourselves. The bed shook and we refused
to be shaken off. Your slip trembled toward
the edge of the chair and over, your dress
after, my shirt, pants, socks. The light
flickered and did not go out entirely.
As flakes of paint began to cover us,
we gasped and did not let go. I'm not sure when,
only that we fell asleep. Maybe you dreamed,
as I did, of a couple on a long voyage,
he by air, she by sea, nothing but cloud
and water around them, no land to be seen.
I dreamed that our bed was moving in the same
direction as their vessel in the dream.

When I woke up this morning, your eyes
were closed, but following something quick
beneath the lids: only then did I know
we had reached solid ground once again.

The Amaryllis Sounds Reveille

and the air hums electric all day
without overheating.
                                        A rooster
in the neighbour's yard, confused
by all the blue light cast by
trees in our orchard, sounds the
alarm from nightfall till dawn.

You also fit into this picture
somehow, turning a spherical dream
over in your hands without waking,
drawing lines on its surface, as if
it were a globe and you had somewhere
to go.
          As always, I play the part
you expect me to play, saying *warm,*
warmer, hot! because the words
have always served to steer you
in a direction you could not fault.

But now, like you, I have no goals:
we watch the apples burn up on
their branches;
                                we listen to the
rooster crow, and that seems enough.

Old Town

In the Alfama, we use what we find
because we will not find it again:
cervejaria, minimercado, woman
in black beneath the photogenic arch.
We accept the rain from the wash
overhead, the geraniums dripping
over the edge of a balcony.
Starting from the top, we wind
left and right and left again,
as the close walls dictate,
the only direction we can rely on: down.
Some alleys announce themselves blind
right away; others make us work
for our knowledge of them. Sudden
church bells break the stucco
from the walls, the laughter breaking too.
You play Gretel, I, Hansel, our parents
far away. *Boa tarde, boa tarde,*
we say to the woman in black, thinking
her own thoughts, the man at the bar,
drinking *aguardente,* not thinking,
or the witchlike creature leaning
out of her low window, still curious
about the world a little. Often
they answer. *Boa noite. Boa noite.*
Only seconds ago, it was afternoon.
The passage still forces us
left and right, winds us down.
On TV, some man and his TV wife raise
their voices; around every corner
their convincing anger increases. Above,
a woman sings a world that keeps
losing itself even as she creates it:
no sooner does a man meet a woman
than he yearns for his freedom;

the woman's face, in the song,
hardens at the thought of her sons
putting out to sea, her daughters
finding husbands who beat them
or no husband at all. We stand
beneath the balcony and listen,
the moment already disappearing.
We will not find it again. *Boa noite.*
We follow the broken steps down.
The wash, you say, *dripping*
on our heads. The geraniums, too,
I answer, trying to remember
where we have been. The buildings
lean into one another, ready to drop.
We pass through, holding on
to each other, whatever we can.

Harvest

The pears on the ground do not
hold still, overripe,
animate yellow.

He yanks his hand away
from a handful of sudden
wasps, drunken.

The bucket she has filled
with plums begins to shiver,
animate blue.

She lets it drop, the wasps,
visibly now, after the soft
flesh scattering.

For years, they have come away
from here empty-handed; of course
they will do it again.

Crosswords

Sibelius, she says, the Finnish composer,
which he did not need to know at eight
in the morning, the letters of the name
a major key to the puzzle and, who knows,
the fact may prove useful again. The echo
of the church bells keeps taking a shortcut
through his head, as does her definition
of some invisible ache or some other
of which he is the most likely cause. Funny,
she says, I read Sibelius, when the label
on the package says Sibelium, medicine
for dizzy spells, whatever centres in
the inner ear: bells, the bells. He tries
to imagine himself listening, hammer, anvil,
stirrup, to the bells, clappers and bells
and the voice for the rest of his life,
working out answers to all the questions
she could ever pose, shouting in triumph
at the paper's crossword bested daily: facts
never more than factual, dates, places of birth,
marriage and death, the intimate voices, say,
for string quartet. The ache remains invisible,
spreading from one of them to the other,
assuming its forms, impossible to pin down
in seven or eight letters exactly. Si-be-li-us,
she says, Si-be-li-um, she says and says
until he listens and her balance returns. She puts
her glasses on to study possible side-effects
of the medicine, the music. Some things refuse
to fit into language. Churches, he says,
should haul down their bells, give it a rest.
A silence, she says, in music, four letters, thank you.

Queluz Palace

In the great hall of mirrors,
among the cut crystal and the gold
and the angels painted on the ceiling,
you flung out your arms all at once
and began to spin in circles,
in wider and wider circles
across a marble floor where Dom Pedro
had danced with Dona Maria, his future queen,
and I could hardly believe my eyes,
though you danced in every mirror
and on every facet of glass and on each
of the marble tiles on the floor
and in the gold, and the best angel
slowly peeled away from the ceiling
to fly, after long years of waiting
just for that moment (it was before noon
on August 3, 1986) and no matter
how I pinched myself or rubbed my eye,
he did not stop swinging you round
in wider and wider circles,
as I stood by, stupefied, stupid,
only watching helpless, and your feet
slowly rose from the polished marble
and you floated, in a straight line now,
out of the hall with the angel,
toward one of the smaller chambers,
which not even the king's own servants
had ever been allowed to enter,
toward a room without glass or gold
where, mercifully, I could not watch you.

Airborne

'A writer is someone who hates himself
and loves the world.'
—Jakov Lind, *Travels to the Enu*

Earthbound, solo, he flies overhead, reluctant
to let go of a world to which he's become too attached:
the trees on Cook Street shedding chestnuts and leaves,
the brown mulch on Gonzales, Garry oaks angled inland
by winds that prevail, and carriages driving through them,
stuffed with tourists happy to cling to whatever memory
the guides can articulate, the pilot not hearing,
but recalling as his Cessna drones a background,
fuel gauge constant on empty and motor stuttering along
the waterfront, through pockets of thin and thick air,
over smoke from a ferry in no hurry to part from the wharf,
going nowhere, and he flies low above the circle of lights
and back to the inner harbour, the park, sudden black spaces
he's more and more absorbed by, letting mind and body go
into them, thinking memory a kind of imagination,
then forgetting who said it, compounding the failure,
his agitation drowned by the engine running on nothing
but vapours, lights steady below, sure sign of insomniacs
at work or calling their work into question, then muttering
to themselves or their drowsy partners because
they've turned 21 or 33 or 40 or 65, whatever the force
of such numbers dictates, the century turning too,
while the world persists, its pebbles and mountains, leaves
and forests, couples in them and on them, the Cessna dipping
and jolting over the different airs that provide a cover,
its pilot aware of the uneasy balance of presence and absence
and names for that, *saudade*, nirvana, heartache, *Weltschmerz*,
tristesse, lovesick singing along to the blues on his radio,
or fado of star and stone, wood, black air, the leather seat
and aluminum frame passing the engine's vibration through,
piston and wing, stroking and being stroked, yes, by air,
cloudy, wet, lights beneath flashing, extinguishing,

and he comes up breathing again, head bursting with colours,
pulls on the throttle till the plane responds, engine sucking
the fumes more efficiently, brings it higher to regard
the city whole, patterned roofs fitting into a near-pattern
of forest and water, fissures of pavement not marring it
from on high, traffic below, drivers without maps, though
from up here no desperation shows, so he veers on impulse
through clouds over to Moss Street, circles and holds,
circles and holds, from the art gallery down to Clover Point
and around again via Beacon Hill Park, James Bay and up
over Fort Street's one-way antique shops, nearly stalls
over the gallery, its Emily Carrs and oriental prints,
some by Hokusai, and the Shinto shrine that will not help
him relinquish the world, too beautiful, as is the blossoming
of cherries along Moss Street the children playing there
ignore, and over our house, the two of us holding on
to each other again, startled by the plane's noise, sudden
into our lives, as the pilot — wasn't he my invention —
angles off on his own over the straits, tuning his radio
to every signal ever sent into the air, weather reports,
religious broadcasts, calls from fishermen to their wives
and daughters, fisherwomen adrift, poets from the sixties
and seventies on the CBC, CB operators and their argot,
impulses, convincing ping of directional signals, English
of international pilots requiring permission to hold
their pattern or land, even as he traverses the city
and islands, randomly stringing together the lights below,
cabin cruisers and freighters sending out a constant static,
as if speaking to him, with their calls keeping in touch
with solid ground, hanging on every word as he rides the air
wherever it takes him, learning the heat coefficients,
the updrafts of ripening corn or cabbage, cooler forests
carrying him to the false dawn and its promise
of more genuine light behind Mount Baker he races toward,
believing, strobe lights on his wing a small echo,
back to the city to buzz its inhabitants over breakfast,
or just starting up from love or insomnia, lovers
and the sleepless alike quizzical, and each partner

or spouse, too happy or sullen to speak, lets out or lets in
the cat and pays scant attention to the pilot overhead,
so low now he can almost gaze into their eyes or down
their hastily tied morning coats, into that promising shadow
from which he thinks he can reconstruct everything—
the tossing of sheets or yanking them over, off the shoulder
that turns all at once cold, and he closes his eyes a minute,
automatic pilot on, to dream again the newspaper story
of a Chinese woman who, having wrestled with a python,
bit it to death, and in hospital now she's shedding her skin,
Tiresias also entering the dream as the pilot shifts
in his own skin, uneasy inside it, wanting to sleep
a deeper sleep or let go the controls, shut the engine down,
but far from those troubled centres of China and Greece,
he turns his plane instead to his own neighbourhood,
each chimney, each pigeon or gull on the roofs a point
that fixes memory, every woman walking below or running
a possibility he pursues to its happiest, most improbable
conclusion, a frost on the black rooftops, thinnest ice
for the sun to burn off, and he imagines his love's
bathroom window mist over, denser and denser steam
he plunges into, to come up gasping, babbling for all
there was and was not to see, his plane passing
through clouds that remind him of his early love for fog,
narcissistic, that strips the world of its shapes,
reattaches them to those lost in it, while the loved one
steams narcoleptic in her bath, soaks without a thought
in the world, unless it's of a lover floating above,
and the pilot lifts his plane through clouds toward
her half-open arms, imagined opening wider to receive him,
laughing, high on his thoughts, not letting go the fogged-in,
clouded-over, rained-on, clean-washed world, flier
that he is, leaper through space, through remembered noise
of all the approvals, praised first step, first word,
sugar and fruit of first schooldays, every memory
leaving him its own sweet time to dwell on, invent anew,
drawing him back to that young mother who'd begun to suckle
her infant before he could find the words to approve,

the engine revving now, him going along, one again, mouth
stuffed, the memory stuck there, sweet, soft as the fog
and warmer, white, all his pulses soaring, the plane
shuddering over thinnest air, soothing and waking him
gradually into himself, space toward which he's flown day
and night, and so he circles through morning, discovering
the structure of paper routes that link all those
who read him up here, without fuel or flight plan and,
eyes closed, he turns to a past into which he slots himself
well enough, there chases a teenage girl for miles
down a gravel road, potholes, black water, the girl
nearly invisible, but he keeps his focus on the chain
and cogs of her bike, black oil on the hem of her skirt,
tires ballooning, and every potential meeting place
saturated with remembered smoke and grease of french fries,
an odd setting for first words of love that he tries
to reform now into a simpler sentence, one imposed
on everyone and so losing its simplicity, but without
a way to restore the balance, without better words,
his thoughts fall into their own indecipherable patterns,
make him steer into another terrain where he finds
the immigrant artist in his basement as usual, discovering
forms for his nightmares of Stettin, Szczecin, places
and their names mutable too, shapely women assembling
and disassembled there, winged men after them, acrylic,
oil, a sun or moon often in the picture, adding invented heat
to imagined affair, the trick always to keep it going,
memory, invention, to draw the stuffs of remote worlds
from Prospect Lake, say, from Meadowbrook Road, to fly
overhead and make out half-familiar rooftops or a raft
toward which, on certain mornings, he might be swimming,
this time setting himself an attainable goal, puffing
in his two languages up onto it, shouting, belly out,
fist high, greetings to a fellow pilot likewise refusing
to let go, one who dives through cloud formations
even as he dives through milfoil, history, signals on radio,
TV and in the papers betraying their murderous contradictions
—Christmas Day for the Ceaușescus—visibility 50 km

and a 100% chance of darkness, certainties still useful
to a pilot, though he wants to shed them, if not the world
and his vision of it, the firs tucked into mist
he flies through, nipping their crowns, green of new growth
his propeller shreds, cones lodged in the wing as he drops,
leaning into the controls for a closer look, approaching
zero gravity, that nirvana, associations made more freely,
the language changing quickly, streaming toward him
on the radio or through his senses, analphabetic at first,
shy perceptions that slowly grow spines, real backbone
so to speak and so speak at last, one perception
after another, really soaring now, unlimited possibilities,
moisture on the windshield turning into its proper word,
glass, wiper, smoke stuttering from the exhaust,
exhausted, and even as he closes one circle around the city
to start another, it begins to snow, fat flakes
on the glass white out his vision, absorb all sound
but the engine's vibration up through his bones,
nearly white noise he is not half lost in, the land below
defined by inlets of black water, streams smudging into it,
illegible script someone may, someday, interpret,
and he's off again building snow forts, rolling pressed grass
and gravel and dirt into wet balls for layering, the walls
soon enough up to his knees, his eyes, shut against missiles,
permitting a dream that contains this one, in which he flies
backward into snow, eiderdown beaten, arms thrashing
the angels themselves in a sweat and sexless,
while he's up here giving and taking, flapping his arms,
the ends of his body nowhere if not in this cloud mass
without visible beginning or end, grey matter
imagining itself arriving, yes, while he's afraid
to open his eyes lest the focus be lost, afraid
to keep them shut lest the body vanish forever,
flying at who knows what altitude and surely climbing,
body and brain soaring into blue that changes
to a bluish black that can absorb anything, cloudlike,
and then it is only night again, the heart slowing,
slowing to one beat and then another, and as he drifts above,

someone invents him below, posits plane and lift
and thrust and so sustains him, holds him there
like the Buddhist elephant stuck in mud, language mired
in reason, logic approaching no truth, nothing but clouds
from which he cannot, does not want to extricate himself,
and time still manages to pass, the clouds occasionally
lifting to reveal a man or woman writing him, or writing
each other, time passing too slowly when they only write
and how quickly once their words catch up to them again,
all breath in the mouth, then mouth-to-mouth and breathing
however they can, taking oxygen straight through the skin,
rush of blood making them flush, pores, follicles,
softest inner lip, breathing aloud, breathing in that rhythm
which is one of the measures of time, unreliable,
while the skin, a no more certain measure of space,
barely contains them, holds the various shapes they try out
on each other, testing limits that appear to vanish
for a pilot dreaming, his fuel tank empty, his heart full
as he wonders how many times he will need to repeat it
to keep himself aloft, and the couple coupling,
image of which he cannot free himself, their cries
a constant static on his radio, impossible to ignore,
impossible breathing, and his stomach grumbles, empty
as the fuel tank, the body also running, so he turns
his plane toward the strait to have body and mind
stop craving awhile, to deal instead with the end that nears,
of flight or the slow millennium gasping its last gasp,
forcing a tally of the defeats, the depletions,
the unsustainable growth of doom and gloom, as befits
a *fin de millénium*, though this does not explain
why he feels so ... up, so ... high, these words
failing also, his plane strafing newly seeded mountainsides,
the timid greens of a better dream and none to share it
as he heads south toward the familiar roofs of those he loves
in his own way, at a distance, keeping roof and air
between them, flying alone at night, drawn to first light,
moth to flame, to shadows or movements in windows, flashes
of women or men and then darkness again, the familiar

tricks of light that make him feel like a sucker, taken in
by carny shows in the fifties, policewomen with folded hands
on their laps as the strippers only begin to unravel,
billboards, promised image and flesh, lit up briefly,
then obscured again, strobed unconscious, and soft only
in the brain, each year softer, the body a fleeting thing,
consciousness tagging along, part air that sustains it,
part metal parts that keep the machine functioning,
and he gives in to his urge to express it — Christ! —
acid or booze loosening the tongue, rambling on innocent
and confused and not yet emptied, while in the morning light
new crowds form below, as if charting their lack of direction
collectively, maybe waiting for someone like him to drop
out of the air with the word, or scatter it on leaflets,
and he circles ever along the one side of his flight,
Möbius strip, avoiding conclusions, amoebic, this flight from
and toward a kind of nirvana, holding on a version
of letting go, everything up in the air, as he is, flying
without fuel, head gone calm at last, all the world now
in one ear and out the other, eye nostril skin tongue,
air pressing over and under the wing, vapour that lifts him
up among the radio signals and not receiving them,
the airport's sporadic warnings, and each replay
of the hourly news which the tiny roar of his engine enters,
repeating itself inside the larger roar of his cockpit,
nothing between, condition to which a part of him aspires,
attraction of glass for glass and a source of light, even
as the rest of him flies from it, the changing levels
of oxygen not clearing his head, the brain never sated,
never free of it, lungs working the miraculous exchange
to absorb it, what little there is in these precious airs,
head firm on the shoulders, eyes without wool over them,
ears ringing but alert to the engine's variations, body also
running on nothing and toward it, mind cleared of longings,
perfect witness that gives everything back unaltered,
leaving the moss on trees and the mushrooms untrampled,
leaving all the virginities intact, leaving the students
dreaming beneath their papier-mâché goddess in Beijing

and the Ceauşescus dreaming, adjusting none of it,
and he goes down, clinging a little to the kids in Fairfield
swinging on tires from branches, untroubled by legalities,
blind to the heads of older neighbours behind curtains
or a Cessna stuka-ing down on them, then climbing again,
over the backs of gulls, wax-winged, startling eagles
out of their circular patterns and himself, too,
to ignore the earth, the soil as well as he can, turning
a deaf ear to the buzz and roar of whatever claims
his attention, the mountains nearby, ice, a mother pushing
her child around and around, patient or only resigned,
like him, learning to abandon the need to see everything
imagined and real, letting go the fear of blindness,
taking the constellations as they come and assigning
no names to them, allowing them to rearrange themselves
and letting them go, not wanting the darkness filled,
not needing the silence cluttered with cries of triumph
or loss, approving the lack of approval, not fearing fear,
not loving love, not hating hatred, not thinking thoughts
about thinking, without mouthing words that cannot add up
to truth or falsehood, flying over the world's thin skin
and grazing it lightly, borne by nothing, by air.

Stormy Night

On the street, three in the morning, roughly,
a driver shifts down without double-clutching,
grinds into low gear for his own amusement:
almost enough to wake the dead. The city hums.
Wind. Then more wind, gusts from the west:
on them, a dog howls, howls again, distant.
It can be pictured as some cocker spaniel pup
or beagle, maybe, the runt of the litter for sure.
How can the wind itself be pictured? German
shepherd? Doberman pinscher, all the force
of its body concentrated on the points
of the teeth: impossible to imagine that pressure.
Wind in the various branches in the window
shakes them variously, shakes the stuff off them:
petal, last winter's leaf, berry or twig.
New and old nests ride out the storm, which the eye
does not tire of tonight, all the soft flotsam
backlit by a streetlight beyond the field
of vision, or by some other light. Everything spills
in time into the window frame and the eye remains
fixed by whatever it's attached to. It's hard
to imagine the birds on those branches asleep.
The tail, we assume, of some neighbour's cat
(we *assume* cat!) taps against the door.
By the time the porch light can expose it
for what it is and was, the animal has vanished
into night again. All cats, at night, etcetera
(and whatever else we care to assume). Something
in sleep grinds a large axe. The dog whimpers,
or the wind, as if after remembered prey in dreams,
the furious legs not touching solid ground,
jaw slack as the tongue to allow the hot breath
to issue freely from the sleeping maw. The bodies
in the cemetery across the street do not turn
in their graves, fact that offers no consolation.
The kids we just were have begun kicking down

the headstones, pinning the serious carnations
into their buttonholes, and dancing without joy
over the freshly dug soil. They make love
less often than we like to think and, later,
have their own reasons for not sleeping.

Cappucine Order

In the gap between lamentation and praise,
leaves spin down in their colours and the moss
thickens into green. Ferns passive all summer
all raise their fronds at once. Somewhere behind
sight and sound, beside it: what a better eye
or ear might take in, a hummingbird's or bee's,
stilling the human pulse. It's no exact science,
this relentless gauging of the self's small part
in the passage, cells acting on their codes
or only giving in to them, some tired
of sun and photosynthesis, while others
go about their work, mitosis or meiosis
or only miracle, as if such process could
never stop. Flickers face off by the water,
less intent all at once on what the bark
of oaks may hold than on each other: bobbing
and singing their small repeated note, they break
the flock down into pairs. What the heart does
with this seems to depend on how long it's beaten.
Between bare rock and air, a new fungus grows.
What was hard proves soft again, and easier.

Torschluss*

The air flickers and rises, everything in it.
Breathe it in.
Breathe out.
Let it go.
Stop brooding about how it works on others,
hikers and bikers this first day of summer.
Forget them.
Focus instead on crickets in the bush,
in the rising broom, clicking,
or on the broom's thick blossoming,
its dark pods that spiral open, catapulting
black seeds outward, too quick for the eye,
slow enough for earth and ear.
And the woman ahead, shadowed
by a younger man hot on her trail,
who may or may not remind you of yourself—
if you cannot say what you're after,
take a moment to gather your thoughts.
Consider each of the distinctions between
the woman, her shadow, and you.
Who cares if she rides her bike slowly,
giving and taking her own sweet time?
Don't even begin to pretend it's for you.
Wipe the sweat from your eye.
Lick the salt from your lip.
Let her pedal, backpedal, brake, then push
her bike at less than the young man's speed,
ratchets clicking, tacking into and
out of your line of vision—
no help now from impossible Zeno!

---

* 'Torschluss': literally, 'shutting of the gates'. Closing time. *Torschlusspanik* is the fear among older people that they won't achieve their goals or find a spouse.

Is that what you're thinking?
Let it go.
She's easy to dismiss; shake him off too.
And don't imagine her elsewhere, dangling
first one foot, then the other,
into lake or bath water.
Turn your back on her and your own image
of her meticulously pumiced foot
sliding evenings into its shoe or glass slipper
clacking up the long wood of your staircase
come morning, breaking into your sleep,
kicking through sunlight that angles past
your bedroom window.
Don't believe these promises of heat and light
even if they make you feel decades younger.
Watch out for the easy miracles, stiletto heels
on which your fancy's too gladly impaled.
Let the woman and the man make their own way.
Go halfway home.
Then half of that.
And another half and half again.
And if this way you reach your door,
lock it behind you.
Set the chain.

Seascape with Donkey

Horsetails in the air,
on the water:
roostertails.

And no horses.
And no roosters.

Somewhere must be
the tail of a donkey,
and a tailless donkey
pinned to a wall,
two-dimensional.

Imagine: a real likeness
of a donkey, real pins,
a solid wall.

Anything can be pinned to it:

an oyster-catcher, whistling,
that flies into fog
and is gone

or a freighter that blows
its own horn and slides
out of this world

or the brain itself grasping
these details, holding on.

How one part connects
with another
or fails to connect.

Maybe I'm the donkey
always needing to be
reattached to the same two
or three things on the earth
or the air or the water.

This Morning, Hanging by a Thread

Spiders shook in their webs, caterpillars
inside their tents. They hung on threads, heading
slowly earthward from them. The sun appeared
as if created for nothing but to show off
the monarch's wing. Moonlight, then,
just for moths? we wondered. At breakfast,
the wasps seemed stickier than usual, confused
or irritated by our presence, maybe groggy like us
in the heat. Carnivores, they ignored butter and jam,
conspicuously, and went straight for the meat,
all too attached to its sinew and fat. How seldom,
you said, do we think things through to the end.
The insects made us think again, follow their thread
right down to the ground, down to soil and grass
where lowly crane flies first begin to err
through the brief inevitability of their lives,
unthinking, thinking neither happy nor unhappy.

Mexican Dogs

Perros: already the poets
have made much of you,
not that you're much to behold,
nor that you do much
to stir us to love you or fear.
For the most part, you seem
content to lie in the shade
of walls or cars, and hardly
care if the walls threaten
to come tumbling down
or the cars start up. Passive
in the heat of day and amorous
presumably by night, you leave
the dugs of the *perras* swollen.
Or are you depressive day
and night? Near-suicidal?
When men pass by,
you look up sadly, checking
for the hidden rock.
When women approach
with empty hands,
you look sad also,
but less alone.

Crickets

Solid as the idea
of bells, of the breath,
once they fall silent.

Tropical Snowman

for Eva

A love poem, this, note and admission to you
who painted it, one of its subjects, him (me?)
snowy, bent over not quite backwards in parody
perhaps of what critics might call 'desire'.
For you, no doubt for me, the sunflower only
shines down on him, sun balloon at the end
of the little string he clings to. Too thin.
He offers it to her (I to you), sun or balloon
or aching token of the heart, arcing high
over the other curves you've layered artfully
one over the other, the seeming accidents rendered
deliberate now, brushwork that does not have her
brushing him off (you, me). So I need to think.
This note, like your painting, wants to be
its own illustration, the words, no less
than the paint, a likely cover-up. Can there be
an accurate medium for this? And because
I have read your reading me into your work,
I sketch us into mine also, hopeful, the carrot
of my nose pointing ever toward you,
without compass finding the right direction,
as I think you'd have it. I agree. And
you've given us real arms and legs, not sticks!
Yes, of course it's self-referential — or is it
reflexive? — the cozy vacuum of our lives
promising to keep us warm as coffee or soup,
and me, presumably snow or ice before, now melting
toward you, and you, without pretence to modesty,
claiming those classic lines you have given yourself.
And while you don't return my gaze, neither do you
refuse it. No, this work catches us well enough,
you with your dreams of steamier climates,
me with mine of chasing after you south.

You Deal with the Spirits at Monte Alban

Once we *no-gracias* ourselves past the knickknack peddlers
and offers for personalized tours in any of fifteen languages—

Español no problema, Deutsch bestimmt, Français qui sait?—
and past the difficult ticket-taker irritated by our entry

by way of the exit, and once we take in the first full view
of the architectural and panoramic splendour, and fend off

the descendants of the natives who achieved it and who now
make masks as their ancestors did, of genuine resins derived

from the local trees and who knows what else, *barrato,*
almost as convincing as the partially reconstructed mask

at the Museo Rufino Tamayo far below, and once
we're finally alone at what purports to be the lodging

of a chieftain, a little maze of walls and stone without
the platform on which the athletes gave up their lives

if they won, no skulls chiseled all around, nor what priest
and conquistador thought dancers, you commune with whatever

spirits that touch you in the protective shade of the wall,
while I fuss and fluster over the hibiscus, the hummingbirds,

said to be ghosts of warriors slain in battle, the distant plain
that slowly seems to vanish into its own thickening haze.

Pulling in from the Rocks

Having fooled you, the tide keeps you drifting
toward the rocks with its barnacles, coral,
sea urchins, and me swimming minutes away
with my clumsy fins. In a controlled panic,
you call, just loud and hard enough to suggest
some urgency, not so much that I panic too.

Cramp? Sharks in the water? Jellyfish sting?
My amplified feet get me to you in time,
get us both slowly away from the rocks.

Relax. Put your mask in the water and float.
Let me do the work for a while, for once.

Something about this feels like a reversal.
Usually, I'm the one who is drifting, now closer,
now farther away, and never toward nor away
from anything so solid as rock.

You're the one who nudges me ahead or pulls me
back in. Relax. Relax for once and see: for all
your hard-earned doubts, it's still working.

Table Talk

> 'A man desires and longs after things
> that are uncertain and of doubtful result,
> but condemns that which is certain, done,
> and accomplished.'
> —Martin Luther

More and more of the days we spend talking
about the days gone by in which nothing
memorable happened, making it easy
to bicker about the details that, like
memory itself, grow in importance. Once,
decades ago, in the kitchen of a
visiting American poet, you
and I leaned against the fridge all evening,
at a gathering of poets and readers
of poetry, and you and I stood by
the fridge talking anything but. Your name.
The German pronunciation and not
so German sound of it. I kept quiet about
your eyes from which I sometimes lowered mine.
Quiet your breasts. Your hands. Legs. The brown suede
of your miniskirt. The large silver loops
of your earrings which later caught the eye
of a novelist from South Africa;
he caught himself in them as if they were
Möbius strips. Your ears flushed. We talked
of anything but and the details did not
matter so much. Lip, tongue, mouth and so forth.
Words spilled out of my ache only to touch
and you seemed talkative too. The talking
alone seemed to matter. In the living room,
I suppose the poets were heady, heavy
under their influence, gossiping about
who was sleeping with whom, while we bided
our time in the kitchen, only wanting.

Status of the Beggar in Old Havana

Cuba's coffee tastes bitter, *ersatz,*
and the sugar flaked in damp sachets
carries too much history to sweeten it.

Too many sugar barons and their *marquesas*
had crowded their mansions with Meissen china,
Venetian glass, Tiffany's wisteria lamps,
vases from all the dynasties.

Today, their portraits glower at all
who dare visit their *museo* or mausoleum
few can afford to enter. No wonder
this sugar does not taste sweet.

In Old Havana, a blind man taps out
some Afro-Cuban rhythms on a pail
that might have been a flower pot.

Ever more urgent, his fingers drum louder
as the silence of coins provides
the only horizon note.

Tourist-policemen gently lead him away.
We turn to our guidebook, drink coffee,
open sachet after bitter sachet.

An Ideal Place

In this cave, no one needs to drag
his shadow up the wall toward
an elusive sun, no allegorical marker
marks how far we keep falling
short of it.

Slow water dissolves
slow limestone and crystallizes
where once shellfish had worked
on their shells.

Time, wherever it was, has dropped out
of the space-time continuum.

Inconsolable bats flap their wings, vanish
back into the stalactite mysteries,
of which, in this timelessness,
we think we know a thing or two.

Faces. Men. Women. Totemic animals.
Armies marching on cities. Trumpets
raised. Towers rising. Walls collapsing.
The angelic. The earth. The imagined
taking root even as real roots drop
through nothing down to clear water.

We have forgotten almost everything
we have read of Plato and here
that does not trouble us. The small light
far ahead guides us well enough.

Up there, the protected species endure.
Snakes with their innocent poisons fall
from the palms onto the necks
of innocent creatures, in a natural cycle
into which we must surely fit.

About Derk Wynand

Derk Wynand was born on June 12, 1944 — or, as he likes to say, 'not quite a week after D-Day'[1] — in Bad Suderode, Germany, a spa town tucked into the Harz mountains, in Saxony-Anhalt. His father, Jan Wynand, had met his mother, Odette Bergamy, who worked as a secretary, at the Café Kranzler in Berlin in the spring of 1939; someone had suggested that Jan, then an engineering student, could help Odette with her math. After he'd obtained his degree and the war had started, Wynand's father was assigned to Organisation Todt, a civil and military engineering group responsible for Nazi construction projects. At the time of Wynand's birth in Bad Suderode, his parents and Rainer, a brother sixteen months Wynand's senior, lived in nearby Osterode, where Jan was stationed to help build a jet-fuel plant. The Wynands remained there postwar and emigrated to Canada in 1952. Jan crossed the Atlantic six months ahead of his wife and two sons, eventually finding a new life for them and for himself in British Columbia.

From 1952 to 1954, Wynand's family lived in central Vancouver at three addresses while his father 'had a job at Kitimat Constructors and Mom worked in what's now Gastown, at David L. Jones Florists.' In 1954, when Wynand's maternal grandmother joined them, they 'moved into an empty shell of a house' in Surrey. His father, by then working for Timber Preservers (later known as Coppers), headed the engineering division. The Surrey property grew into a small acreage, where his mother raised horses. The quasi-country life of mid-twentieth-century suburban Vancouver is voiced occasionally in Wynand's early poems.

Though Wynand had intended to become a chemist when he registered at the University of British Columbia in 1962, he graduated with a double major in English and philosophy in 1966, even though his 'best subjects had been French and math'; in his final year, he took an introductory creative-writing course. In early 1967, he moved to Toronto, then to Quebec, where he taught English at the Berlitz School of Languages in Montreal and Drummondville. By September he was back west to start an MA in creative writing at UBC, where he studied with J. Michael Yates and Michael Bullock, who 'steered [their students] toward translation'.

When Wynand arrived in Vancouver in 1952, 'a kind grade-1 teacher' took charge of him and his brother until they spoke English well enough to join their respective grade 3 and 4 classes. The brothers soon replied to their parents' German in English; by the time their maternal grandmother died in 1963, they all mostly spoke English at home. The struggle to retain his birth language became a concern that would also shape his reading and his poetry. 'My grandmother guiding my fountain pen through homework assignments for hours, then painstakingly scratching out the errors with a small pocket knife,' writes Wynand in a paper he gave at Germanica 88, a conference held in Vancouver in April 1988, 'is for me the ultimate image of the difficulties of language — the first language.'[2] When he was an MA student, 'Michael Bullock shocked me when he told me that my translations of French were better than those of German. I had assumed I knew German, and so used fewer dictionaries and reference books than I did with French.'

In 1968, Robin Skelton accepted Wynand's translation of Chatard's 'Jarnacueira' for publication in *The Malahat Review*, the University of Victoria's year-old journal. His MA obtained in 1969, he began to teach writing in UVic's Department of English and, initially, while he continued to write and translate poetry, he also translated German radio plays, even trying his hand at writing a radio play himself, for broadcast on the CBC. In 1973, when Creative Writing broke away as a separate department, Skelton invited him to be the *Malahat*'s assistant editor. By Wynand's own admission, he shared 'Robin's internationalist view of poetry.' On the strengths of his Artmann translations, Skelton asked him to edit 'Austrian Writing Today'; Artmann's publisher provided Wynand with introductions to prominent Austrian writers, and he contributed many of his own translations of their work to the issue, which appeared in 1976. Its publication marked the end of his first 'stage' as a *Malahat* board member. He enjoyed a second brief stint as Constance Rooke's associate editor in the mid-1980s and, at her instigation, he applied to replace her in 1992, staying at the helm of the magazine until 1998. Though teaching and the administrative underbelly of university life often took a toll on his writing, Wynand 'loved the give and take of [creative-writing] workshops.... I hated giving lecture courses, being more full of doubt than certainties, though at least my doubts and self-doubts gave me a good sense about what many of my students were experiencing, something that I think let me help the best of them to keep going.' The best included Patricia Young, Jillian Wigmore, and Warren Heiti. The most enjoyable 'times were office hours, one on one in the office or the cafeteria, when my students taught me.' Wynand retired as a full professor from the Department of Writing, which he had chaired twice, in 2004.

Within months of joining the University of Victoria, Wynand met his wife, Eva Carr (née Kortemme). Born in Münster, Germany, in 1940, she grew up in Hildesheim. Forbidden by her father to study art, she 'got accepted into UCLA' in 1965, where she planned 'to continue her studies in sociology but got distracted by the lifestyle — and did some modeling.' Coming to Victoria with her first husband, Jerry Carr, who joined UVic to teach physical education and who remained a lifelong family friend, she met Wynand at a party on November 16, 1969. Their married life, which began on May 8, 1971, involved countless mutually supportive intimacies, with Eva helping him preserve and deepen his German, a mastery that found perhaps its fullest expression in his translations of German-born, Finnish-based poet Dorothea Grünzweig. In 1986, while they were on sabbatical in Portugal, food poisoning left Eva bedridden for a week. 'I got her a notebook and a bunch of coloured felt pens that led to ... the rebirth of her ambitions as artist,' a long-frustrated vocation leading to exhibitions, sales to collectors, and a prolific, three-decades-long career. Their time in Portugal also spurred Wynand to write the poems in *Heat Waves*, his fifth book, setting a model for writing based on travel that took him and Eva to Mexico and Cuba. The poems that their many visits south inspired would anchor his next three collections. In 2015, Eva was diagnosed with cancer; she died on November 15, 2019, one day short of the fiftieth anniversary of the day they met.

1. Unless otherwise indicated, all quotations are drawn from Wynand's replies to questions I posed to him by email in February and June 2020.
2. 'My German Heritage', a paper presented at Germanica 88, Vancouver, April 23, 1988, p. 4.

A Bibliography

POETRY

Snowscapes. Delta: Sono Nis, 1974.
Pointwise. Fredericton: Fiddlehead Poetry, 1979.
Second Person. Victoria: Sono Nis, 1983.
Fetishistic. Erin: Porcupine's Quill, 1984.
Heat Waves. Lantzville: Oolichan, 1988.
Closer to Home. London: Brick, 1997.
Dead Man's Float. London: Brick, 2002.
Past Imperfect, Present Tense. Calgary: Bayeux Arts, 2010.

POETRY CHAPBOOKS

Locus. Fredericton: Fiddlehead Poetry, 1971.
Airborne. Victoria: Outlaw, 1994.
Door Slowly Closing. Victoria: Hawthorne Society, 1995.

FICTION

One Cook, Once Dreaming. Victoria: Sono Nis, 1980.

TRANSLATIONS FROM GERMAN

H.C. Artmann, *Under the Cover of a Hat / Green-Sealed Message.* London (UK): Quartet, 1985.
H.C. Artmann, *Sweat and Industry.* London (UK): Atlas, 1992.
H.C. Artmann, *The Quest for Dr. U.* London (UK): Atlas, 1993 (co-translated with Malcolm Green).
Erich Wolfgang Skwara, *Black Sails.* Riverside: Ariadne, 1999.
Dorothea Grünzweig, *Midsummer Cut.* Ottawa: BuschekBooks, 2002.
Dorothea Grünzweig, *Glass Voices Lasinäänet.* Ottawa: BuschekBooks, 2004.